LINZIE

Jared

KYLe

Greg

RYDENDUHL

Brian

TORO

Michael

Eisha

KRISten

CATHERINE Amanda

Renee

Corky

Katie

Cristal

Cassie

KATRINA

Bonnie

LET'S TAKE A WALK ON THE
BEACH

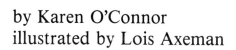

by Karen O'Connor
illustrated by Lois Axeman

THE CHILD'S WORLD

ELGIN, ILLINOIS 60120

Distributed by Childrens Press, 1224 West Van Buren Street, Chicago, Illinois 60607.

Library of Congress Cataloging in Publication Data

O'Connor, Karen.
  Let's take a walk on the beach.

  (Five senses walk series)
  Summary: Gordon's day is filled with delight as he uses his five senses to appreciate the many aspects of a visit to the beach.
    1. Senses and sensation—Juvenile literature.
[1. Senses and sensation. 2. Beaches] I. Axeman,
Lois, ill. II. Title. III. Series.
QP434.035 1986   612.8   86-9551
ISBN 0-89565-354-0

1 2 3 4 5 6 7 8 9 10 11 12 R 93 92 91 90 89 88 87 86

LET'S TAKE A WALK ON THE
BEACH

"We're here; we're here," Gordon
shouts. He runs across the sand,
looking at the blue, blue water.

Gordon likes the beach. There are so
many things to see.

There are
    big boats and little boats
    tied to a pier.

There are
    rowboats and motorboats,
    sailboats and houseboats,
    all kinds of boats.

Gordon sees sea gulls flying overhead,
looking for fish. . .

a fat lady and a thin girl under a big
umbrella. . .

a man with a mustache and a boy with
red hair, building a sand castle. . .

an old lady in a straw hat, collecting
seashells. . . and two boys playing catch
with a Frisbee.

After a while, Gordon lies down. He
likes the cool feel of the damp sand
against his body.

He also likes the hot, dry sand. He likes to touch it with his fingers. . .

with his toes. . .

and his feet.

Most of all, Gordon likes the cool
water and the hot sunshine.

"Look, Mom, I can float," he calls.

Running along the beach, Gordon
looks for shells. He looks under
slippery green seaweed and all along

the water's edge. He finds all sizes
and shapes of shells.

As Gordon walks along, he hears
sounds all around. Sea gulls flap
their wings. A dog barks at the birds.

Boys and girls splash in the surf.
Waves crash on the shore.

Gordon hears a small sail flapping in
the wind. . .

hears the chug-chug of a big
motorboat . . .and from a distance,
the sound of a tugboat's horn.

"I need some suntan oil," Gordon
says, as he smells it melting on bare
backs.

He also smells salty, sea water. . .

juicy burgers and hot dogs, frying on
grills. . .

and hot buttery popcorn, popping at
Jack's Snack Shop.

Gordon runs up to the little window.
He stands on his tiptoes. "One box of
popcorn and one lemonade," he calls to
the man inside.

Gordon is hot and thirsty. The icy-cold, sweet, tangy lemonade tastes great. He drinks it fast.

Then he walks back to the end of the
pier, eating the hot buttery corn. The
sun is going down. The sea gulls swoop
and call.

Gordon's parents fold up their big, blue beach towel. Gordon sits quietly waiting.

"I like the beach," Gordon says. "I hope we can come again soon."